Girl running

Girl running

DIANA HOPE TEGENKAMP

Thistledown
Press

Thistledown Press Ltd.
P.O. Box 30105 Westview
Saskatoon, SK S7L 7M6
www.thistledownpress.com

Library and Archives Canada Cataloguing in Publication

Title: Girl running / Diana Hope Tegenkamp.
Names: Tegenkamp, Diana Hope, author.
Description: Poems.
Identifiers: Canadiana 20210184981 | ISBN 9781771872140 (softcover)
Classification: LCC PS8639.E37 G57 2021 | DDC C811/.6—dc23

Cover and book design by Marijke Friesen and Diana Hope Tegenkamp
Cover image: Getty Images
Printed and bound in Canada

Thistledown Press gratefully acknowledges the financial assistance of
The Canada Council for the Arts, SK Arts, and the government of Canada
for its publishing program.

For
Elizabeth (Betty) Tegenkamp
1940 – 2018

Contents

SPECTRA

the tenacity of light I've witnessed slant

through tree branch and windowpane

onto living room wall—

buoyant shadow-shape lung

exhaling a star-point bloom

not far behind, accordion ribcage shimmer

fibrous orange, trembling

heading northwest

I pick up the camera

frame the landing-place

the ongoingness of *I see you*

Frequency

What if it's complete?

Maybe light

    doesn't seek anything.

The honeybee's dark shape,
the river's leafed estuary,
gutted sky.

Things seen.

Flametop Green,
   Abandoning the Wedding.

The names of songs.

Because to say "you" is to think

of the two great arteries

carrying blood to the head.

How the hand uncurls.

As if the palm
could open and cup "the heart."

As if circles of sunlight could warm

the berries of the mountain ash
in snow.

My seven-year-old nephew tells me:

"Aunty, my brain is blank. Everything
I learned last year in school has been erased."

Pressing his fingers to his forehead:

"Erased."

There are words for fingertips and weekdays.

For moss, starfish,
        and grieving.

What about words that break
        the river's crust of ice,

                press my hand to your chest,

            its warbled, two-time
                slipstream?

What about so much light

        the mind goes white?

Little Winters

1

Sparrows thrum in denatured vine,
      anticipating sunlight.

My mother's gaze steadfast
        even though winter,
its weighted banks,
drift inside her left eye,
        morning seen through
        snow granules.

2

Steadfast,
      another gaze,

the face of María Salguero
glowing white in front of her screen
    as she marks desert locations
      on her digital map,

all those silent sand dunes,
    weighted curves.

3

Head tilted, my mother considers
southwest ice-melt corner,
      snow accumulation on roof,

how to paint a prairie blizzard.

Nakaya, too, winter-obsessed,
      created 3,000 photographic plates

snowflakes
his muse.

4

Vapour figures form in the ice

      along the river's edge
      after a day of sunny weather.

Look, my mother says, look,

pointing at their abstract shapes
      strangely branching.

5

White blur,
      snow slippage

from roof,

     and little rabbit behind the vine,
attuned
to my window-watching presence,

   gone still.

  This tendency to freeze
in the face of mortality,
day
      suddenly folding in on itself,

for seven minutes,

     those soldiers, held in limbo

     slack-jawed
beneath a solar eclipse, 585 BC.

6

She told me how, in Grade One,
    she ran away
again,
       and again.

Loved to tell about her grandfather
returning to the house after walking her to school
only to find her, already back,
sitting on the couch,
as he came through the door.

7

Each evening,

María Salguero
pinpoints last moments
        in the Sonoran
        and Chihuahuan deserts.

Steadfast, all those beloveds.

Somewhere, beneath karst and hardpan
all those women who tried to run, couldn't
        get away.

8

That one April when spring withdrew,
went in reverse,
        and I'm crossing the bridge
        in a snow-globe city.

My mother
opens the front door,

        snowflakes floating round her

profound as secrets.

9

Winter, passing. Spring
        approaches.

        The last time
she shoveled,
            the neighbour came over,
        she told him not to worry,
                said:

I love the snow,
        so clean and cold.

10

Hoarfrost tree ribbons
and ice flurries.

I can see her

        running

fast-footed across those fields.

11

        She told me how as a child,

        she was instructed
to mouth the words to songs in the school choir,

because she sang
out of tune.

Winter
        tells no one its business
        builds layers of close-mouthed reserves

resilient
without commentary.

12

Songs, and cries
        held in,

        not voiced.

Our Highway of Tears
and Starlight Tours

                victim impact statements

seismic beneath tar sands
        deep-rooted through winter.

13

        Mouth moving,
masking its own silence
        as it forms

each vowel and consonant.

Eventually, those soldiers, gone still beneath a cosmos
shadowed strange,

called it quits,
went home.

And Nakaya, in love with snowflakes,
turned to frost heaving.

14

Outside the window
January floats.

I search for signs—
sudden cures, can't
help it—

peripheral drift
in my mother's left cancer eye,

her vision
a wind-tossed sea.

Morning light on building,

reverse Titanic rising.

Loop

Invented histories, extinct species of butterflies, and languages, branching exile. The rise and fall of piano notes, computer's hum, and backroads where the wind blows clean through. Pattern of pink blossoms on my living room chair and the animal nature of letters, forming, begetting, coupling tactile experience and supple thinking. A century emptied and absolute, the open cavity of your chest. The human species learning to undo the knot of otherness and the ringing of a cell phone made in Juárez, Mexico. What does the dawn know of dark woods? Or the desert where the hands of a girl reach through the air? Somewhere on the Tajapuru River in Brazil, the children tie their canoes to big boats. Outside Saskatoon, a dark-haired woman opens a car door and runs. Close up, our features disappear. How humanity must flee from itself. Every day I'm writing this letter, standing in front of the sea. No, a wheat field beneath a sky of stars. This year, how much rain will fall? Tell me that. Tell me the rose, after it's bloomed and before and the blooming. How it's connection, mutual caressing of faces, hands. Long after you've risen without the word lavender to describe your footsteps in snow. A woman walking the white bone alley, skein of solitude entangled in hope and dreaming.

ARTERIAL

… I say yes, I say all of it yes …
NICOLE BROSSARD

it's that story about getting lost

on a familiar country road

junction you never found

perspective with no end

all those gravel years

billowing out behind the car

The Return

DESCENT

Speedometer glows
in my dream.
Blurred rabbit bounds across blue dusk.

My hands crank the wheel
and the car launches
over the edge.

I wake to pain.
Hands to ears.
Chew gum. Cry. Swallow.

Montréal-to-Saskatoon.
Stopover: Toronto.
Nothing prevents the plane's descent.

GROUND

Mom's "Hi" in my ear as we hug at the airport.
My sisters already cracking jokes.

On the three-hour ride across the prairies
we mark locations with sentences.

"There's a gopher."
"Farmers are planting their winter wheat."
"Should we stop for coffee in Watson?"

Alongside this car ride, a Noir Western film plays,
starring my first father's ghost,
galloping on a ghost horse over the prairies.

As we pull into the restaurant, I set my fedora
at a jaunty angle, turn, and deadpan my line: "Grief
comes here like anywhere else, Mister.
One road at a time."

Through the kitchen window,
dark pines rise from the mollusk dawn.
Mom washes, I dry.

"Try for balance."

MINUS 45 WITH WIND CHILL

Last night my favorite figure skater
drifted into my dreams on the dry night air.
Hey, I said.

We walked across a green meadow,
his arm round my shoulder,
as he told me about his secret child
and bought me a coke.

6 AM, frost ferns across the window.
Radio Announcer 1: *And the temperature today
is minus-45 with wind chill.*

Radio Announcer 2: *But next week*
we're going to be in the plus-es—
the plus-es!

Today I will get out of bed.
Eat sensibly. Exercise.
I call Mom about borrowing

her cross-country skis.
The park, she says,
it's only a block away.

That line from Buffy the Vampire Slayer
plays in my mind: *the hardest thing to do*
in this world is to live in it.

I lie back in bed.
Thoughts of Montréal
perfectly formed parasols.

Morning surges
over the riverbank.

BODY

Covered in hives for five days.
Go to the hospital—not once, but twice.
Legs, arms, torso
a map of raised red continents.

Purged on steroids, sleep.
Dream winding streets

light brushstroked
around every corner.

Think to yourself:
been here before.
Polifora windows, rhythmic arches—

and streamlined forms
crisscrossing
beneath the canal's surface.

Take photographs.
Not studied portraits, but delight,
blurred in silver nitrate, and

just like that
you're no longer separate.
You're waves and filaments,

one great arrow pointing
away from the Ebro
and the Strait of Gibraltar, towards oxygen.

You follow the gentle slope downward,
past Amphihelia and Lophohelia,
past Crinoid sponges with open arms

like orchid petals,
towards the ocean bottom.
Feed on a profusion of succulent flesh.
You rest there, in darkness.

HOPE

Pelicans with valour
and recklessness
brave the overflow weir.

Snow in May,
I long for a firm jaw line
by June.

Everyone freaked over the Michael Jackson documentary.
The week before, it was the space shuttle disaster.
News as carnage.

Winter cups its ice hand
and lifts me above
the toboggan hills.

Trees
after Robert Hass

Autumn leaves
at the point of falling.

Readiness and decay.
Then the chickadee's fee bee.

Traveler, where are you going?

    *

In front of me, twenty-one children,
short, tall, dark, pale,
voices rise to a single note—

then off they file; the mother next to me
a hairdresser; I ask her
if she works a lot. Not too much,
she says. Music-box voices
filter from the practice room.

A man in a suit, this week's
rehearsal volunteer, stuffing newsletters
into folders, father, maybe, to the tiny girl
with glasses, or the dark-haired boy.

    *

Slanted rays on a Thursday afternoon
an opaque curtain around the United Church on Third,

windswept passage to the bridge and tossing leaves
of poplar trees down 5th Avenue.
A crow lands on a lamppost and cries out.

                    *

They're bold, like splashes of ink, crows.

                    *

Leaves descend,
dream's twin.

Sharp, the cold touched me last night,
dry leaves along the sidewalk,
alley leaf-deep,
house dark and seeing Mom
coming up the front walk
with the dog, and then the lamp
reflects on pictures and windows
and light draws its furrow
through my gut and heart.

                    *

Enticing to dream
the spaces between leaves
on a Thursday afternoon
to be between thought for a while
the silent part of song.

                    *

Sun, pale liquid through slats of blinds,
trees outside bare. Light passing
hard to hold onto, harder to see.

*

Last night uncovered
sudden sounds.
First, three bells ringing
then overhead an airplane.

No, not a plane.

                Wind,
and a black-haired girl running in a field.
She isn't hope dressed in blue, or faith
darting around in running shoes.
She's a girl.

*

After Hass,
and for Brossard:

Yes, I open the door to the spare room
in the southeast corner, facing towards the river,
legless chairs, lamps, and the insistent scent
of cardboard boxes and newspaper, rose paperweight
and kinship statue, candle sconces, tubes of color,
paintbrushes, rustle of fabric, creak of old hardwood.

My eyes translate the sky,
late geese linked in fluctuating V's
the colour orange desiring the trees.

Clouds

        My father's green Pontiac
carrying him north over highways and gravel roads,
low horizon binding dark to day, and day
to all those foolscap sheets
in a vinyl suitcase on the back seat. Dreams, he knew,
could be better than the dreamer. Sure,
he abandoned the cause, yet he kept
writing and visiting his mother in the tent
by the nuisance grounds until he died in that hotel room.
Quick, I'm told, his burial.

        *

In the spare room, photographs,
handwriting on the back, names
I don't know. The light has shifted, bare branches
tubes of gold. Tubes of light, traveling towards the sky.

        *

Dusk beyond the pine trees and
his mother's expression, an impasse.
Then she cut off
her braids. Later, in poems,
phrases and words underlined,
his shock came to the surface. This was
1958 but already the sixties, wind-blown,
had found him.

After her funeral, moments returned
in brief flashes, here and there. He gathered these smallest parts of her
inside him. To cry might release them,
so he drank, a reverse river
of grief that kept her close.

          *

Strange, how the wind can disperse
thought, lift monuments
of tenderness, buried in darkness.
                    Yet the submerged world
                    isn't life, life is breath
and waking.

The Czech poet says, "I am here."
I look at the vase
of white zinnias on my computer table.
The color white always makes me think
of my sister. Her urgency, its bright flame.
We were listening to
Joni Mitchell's Both Sides Now, kids running in and out, walls
freshly painted blue. Closeness doesn't require
the hush of night or deep talk. I used to
colour her hair like the sun in an autumn afternoon.
Today's sky is grey and blue, why speak
to the dead? Let them return in dreams
if they must. This morning, go down to the river.
Touch the tree trunks and tell the clouds:
I see you.

Birthmarked

1.

Dawn is buffalo in the fog,
because buffalo is the sweetest part of it.
I sit at the desk in front of the window,
the chief's messenger, east smudged between concrete.
On the other side of the river, Mom is reading
in her chair, her little dog at her feet.
Dawn is the half-moon speckled by tawny dark,
because moon is the closest I can get to it.

2.

That plume of sound, night's ancestral keening.
D. H. Lawrence calls them terrifying,
the under-deeps,
because they are not known.
When I'm wakened by my dad
doing his hiyahiyahi from the grave,
I'm not scared, I'm dumbfounded.

3.

The coming of summer,
walking the length of tree belt,
July's dark brown forewing of commitment
feathering our skin with ochre light.

We are two irregular transverse rows of emotions,
mother and daughter, half-touching,
alighting, in the outer half of morning.

4.

Wind stirred dust from ditches
the night he was taken
slouched against hard vinyl car seat
low moon and his mother's face merging
in stuttered sleep.

After beatings, they let him go and he sought
the blue spruces behind the school. Looking up, through branches,
darkness run through with bright patches,
she came to him then, summer-burnished, gap-toothed.

Time, its weight and wing, he stitched
to his shoe, intermittent flight.

That afternoon, he dreamt
rabbit tracks in snow, loping marks
leading to the clearing's edge.
In one hour, winter passed.
In minutes, grief pooled from him,
spring melt.

Curtain lifts, he's there.
Humming some wordless tune as he gets out of the Pontiac,
heads towards her tent.
Dawn's swift hour is a sanctuary lamp
by which he sees this love is mute (though its trick
was to have him think otherwise).

Her hands on his face.
When to speak, when to listen—these things fall away.
Not this motherlove, its selfsame, treeline edge
forms and re-forms within him.

5.

The crocuses are sleeping, not far away,
and I am too, on the couch, half-dreaming
that day the moon eclipsed the sun, what
we fought about forgotten as we gaped
at the dark circle punch-holed through the heavens.

A moon made for anger's turning.
I wait for this half-dream moon to shift—
it does, rising pale and pink through the window.

Now we're in the kitchen, CBC on the radio.
Mom pours coffee, puts cream and sugar
on the counter. Wipes the sink with a towel.
Time, she says, does not flow in even measures.
Wake slowly.

EACH BREATH AN OAR

The Ark

Sleep is not farmland. It has no boundary. Sleep
is wind passing through and round houses and barns, passing round
and over things in formation and form does not matter, nothing
but sleep and dreaming, nothing, just wind, sleep
and this dream, blurred deer in field at side of road.
Sleep is wind, passing over deer and field, wind-blurred windshield,
your hands release the wheel and the van drifts towards the horizon
where land, softened by blue dusk, becomes the sea.

Land is sea and the sea, asleep. Inside houses
men and women float in sleep, on the sea, drifting.
Dreaming themselves from above, small shapes,
floating, bobbing in water. Dropping like rain,
like pebbles. Voices on the wind, yielding, flying,
dispersing. Then gathered once more. Drifting thread of sea-names.
Cord of wind. Sea-laughter.

To row in the dark, each breath an oar.
In the dark, towards the barn,
lowing moan, calf slipping from its mother's body,
birth fluids that you smear on the cow's muzzle.
To see yourself, bent form kneeling in straw.
To see the cow move toward her newborn.
But not to see it. Round you. Round the barn.
Its grey surround. Each breath an oar,
yet breathing does not pull it forward.

Small boat bobbing, bed afloat, and blue horizontal
sluice of light, blue passing, a retinal scan
over this body on the bed. How strange, to dream,
not asleep. To float, to reach the flow of sleep and
from the well draw breath. Horizon not yet land, blue pooling,
giving way. You're awake, God says,
and already you're forgetting the sea and that something
floating through it all—how could you not?
Thumbprint moon eggshell sky birdsong
through the open window.

In-between

He takes the turnoff to the city. This morning,
everything something else. Thoracic flow
of trees. Highway a lung, breathing mist.
Aether spirit, deer at highway's edge.

Gone

He longed to jump.
I fed him wisdom.
Then we went down to the river.
One second, he was there.
Next, gone into that green
water. The goose came.
Offered silence. All I had to do
was be the pond.

Within

Because of that tree
branching dusk. Because of
the word "chair," lost
and later found. A tulip
enfolded in thought lets go.
That afternoon at the library,
as we placed your books in the bag,
I vanished. In my place,
brown trout, mouth agape
as if to say, I didn't see
this coming. Now feed on me.

Far

You know how to measure yearning
when you know. The raw suffering
of factory animals. What can measure that?
Seeing, a kind of greed. Blue iris
of an eye. Hands on countertop.
How do we know a certain slouch
will cause such surrender? We don't.
Our eyes can't anticipate space collapsing,
can't predict such generosity.

Into

What do you want? I said.
Thought, he said, and our fingers
touching beneath this book.
How will you feel if I give you that?
Strong, he said. I dissolved
my body into nectar and fed him.
Then the wolf came, offered
wildness. Said all I had to do
was think of her and she'd be there.

Geese

Dreamt a dream. Startling against black night,
black land, two white geese.

Two farmers. One played by Paul Newman.
The other, Newman's farm buddy.

The men brutalize the geese.
Grey zone, details blurred, pain immeasurable.

The geese leave behind

their bodies, crushed, at the pond,

change into two crooked ostrich-swans,
and walk the land.

Inside, the ostrich-swans are human,
                        their ligaments and bones

phantom-pained, memory-filled.

It's more than they can bear yet they move on,

their pace slow and measured.

As If

as if the river
as if rising
as if the translucid dawn

as if things are what they are
and not as we would have them
the husband
lament, ecstasy

as if everything tends to perfection
the eclipsed moon and your nieces, parkas
open, bare heads
as if humour
as if the garden and your mother's coffee cup
and a garage full of boxes

as if this walk along the river, and the cormorants
blue ghosts on the telephone wire
pink light and the bridge
bow-shaped, blue

as if the woman walking her two greyhounds
in the morning along the river
the woman
and the dogs and the first snow falling
and the river
blue-bowed, pink-bridged

as if steam rising from the river and the Bessborough
seen through mist through fingers

as if a white rabbit bounding
sixty-five days and two full moons
ragged hair on your neck like a river, like fingers
as if my hands, as if your hair

On the Road near the Crest of a Hill

1

she won't speak about the prairie
(heart-breaking landscape
ghost refractions
wolf, goose, trout, deer, man
emerge, disappear
beneath bowl of sky)

2

unless to say
it has the look of pale butter
except to say the moon
in the clarion sky that night
rose high, brightening the road
wedged between fields grey with silence

3

sunken ditch: green grass
mottled with mud gives way
to the pale-yellow field
its cresting waves an army
abandoning moonlight
retreat into darkness

this, always, the first beginning: life
singing from the muck
unmooring from the field

4

harvesting
like that poet said
"to release the sound"
to concentrate this grasp,
stalk from root
head from stalk, and then
collecting the grain, endlessly

(sunlight gifting wheat
memory-mirage, sound (wind) forming
an O like the missing moon)

5

corn stands sky-high
to children and rabbits
who have the gladness
to munch the pale gleaming flesh
at evening with glee
and sweet hunger

corn stalks, green cobs
kernels marking time
pale yellow resembling
only itself, bright corn

husking one, moist release
of flesh and leaf tearing away—
a generosity

(those moments as a child
scanning horizon
trailer, dog, yellow car
gone, yet out there
somewhere beyond
grass undulations)

6

the answer is to breathe in
that sweet tartness

pale green, spindly hair
warmed by the sun, warm sun
hanging in the place once
occupied by the moon

hand and handful
light, through time, springs

Loop

The necessity of yielding. The sound of a mother's footsteps. Sound of silence. The trickiness of pillows. A draped lamp, and darkness broken by a small square of light. Easy laughter, the impatience of coffee and socks. Boy, do I know socks. And the river, the way steam curls and rises from its black passage. The Bessborough against the skyline and the air vibrating and curious, everything a possible source of energy, reserve, mercy, grace, my heart. Even now in winter, this body of life, sexual work, the cicada, poetry, a wolf turning its ears like radar receivers, the woman, swimming to the surface of his eyes. Her small hands. Her ears. Her cheek. The colors azure, beryl, cerulean, steel, royal. And robin's egg. All blue. Intermittent a word learned in Grade 7 for my eagles, their cries for food from the sky. Bare attentive sea-silent cheekbone. Seashell spiral rough and corrugated. Wax stone frost bone. Resoluteness of a seed, integument of time. The place a loved one was last seen. Sight distilled, tepals, whorls and petals. Sky dream crossing over. Sky empty, walk beneath.

QUARRY

When we speak, we have no choice but to use the terms, putting the relational at risk.

ERÍN MOURE

| my | ~~BELOVED~~ | hist y |

my | *BELOVED*

/ history

~~SINKING~~ my /

~~RELIMINARY~~ ~~WONDROUS~~ | ~~BELOVED~~ / *his*

~~RELIMINARY~~

~~SINKING~~

WONDROUS

| ~~VAPOROUS~~ AVOWEI

VAPOROUS

~~SHAPELY~~ | domed *ice-tipped*

ice-tipped

REMARKABLE,

ABLE,

S SUBJECT UNCERTAIN

CERTAIN

CT | ~~CONTINUED~~

~~OVER-RUN,~~ -WILD ||| **history**

F E V E R E D

F E V E R E D

OVER-RUN -WILD | **history**

Dear—

You who agree *my* | ~~BELOVED~~ | **HISTORY** [2]
should be consulted because it abounds in Wonders
and Contradictions,

2

LETTERS

ON

ANCIENT HISTORY,

EXHIBITING

A SUMMARY VIEW

OF THE

HISTORY, GEOGRAPHY, MANNERS,

AND CUSTOMS,

OF THE

*Assyrian, Babylonian, Median, Persian, Egyptian,
Israelitish, and Grecian Nations.*

FOR THE USE OF SCHOOLS AND YOUNG PERSONS.

BY A LADY.

Anne Wilson.

GLASGOW

1809.

you who plunder

Historical Knowledge, seeking capricious signs, [3]

this import[4] of records[5] is for you.[6]

---

4 Anne Wilson, *LETTER I* (p.4):

REMARKABLE EVENTS (authors

can't agree on how many)

~~AID MEMORY~~

FIX THE ORDER OF TIME.

5

There is no moon tonight.

But night's not always *MOONLESS*.

(see, I've been watching the moon, how

it grows full, then new |appears to hold still |

    | doesn't)

6 On this, can we agree? The **MOON**

(LETTER VII)

shines with a *BORROWED LIGHT*.

First, consider Sappho.[7]

Did she jump?[8]

---

[7] *LETTER XXXVIII* (p. 315)

Wilson tells of her fatal leap

(heartbroken) (over a ferryman)

from ~~LEUCATA~~, the white rock precipice

    (aka **LOVER'S LEAP**) | (also) | ~~LEFKATA~~ |

    (also) |

        | ~~LEUCADIAN CLIFFS~~

[8]

my | ~~BELOVED~~ | **WARNING:**

("the amusement which history affords.") (Wilson, p. 316)

("At all times believe me.") (also, p. 316)

(or did

she

not?)[9]

---

9 | risk |

(((**FABULOUS** | |

(doubt) (joy) (fury) (brilliant characters) |

| true | (leaping) |

| | not true | (*SAPPHO*,

in fact,

was *LEAPLESS*).

Now, consider that mountain[10]

(not far from Lover's Leap) where goats convulsed

    and shepherds, delirious, fell to the ground,

        speaking in broken sentences.[11]

---

10 spewing *hallucinogenic* vapours | (pages 53, 313, 315)

(ethylene emissions) from *PARNASSUS* | **GAEA** |

~~MOTHER EARTH~~

deep |

    | from| her| | | gut

11

Don't you wonder about all those tongue-fevered truths?
Oracular, goatherd glossolalia,[12]
meaning gifted away
    (no records)
        on lonely mountaintops? [13]

---

12 Tonight,

only a **REIGN OF STARS**

transmittting signals | across |

~~UNCERTAIN CENTURIES~~.

13

As you regard the historical arrangement of Time[14],

think often on its Lack of Constant Fullness[15]

ebb (and) flow | | |

rising |

    | declining

---

14 ("...in the time of Perseus, B.C. 168...")

("...till the time of Alexander...") ("...some time after

the battle of Salamis...") ("...in the time of Pausanias and Plutarch...")

("...between the time of Agyges and Cecrops...")

("...who lived | in the time | of Pericles...") (**ABRIDGEMENTS** | are |

                    ~~AIDS | TO | MEMORY~~)

("...at || which time | above | ~~six thou|sand per|sons~~ were ~~slain,~~...")

and ~~thir|ty thou | sand made prisoners~~, and ~~sold as slaves~~..."

15

instruction to themselves,

ANOTHER principal requisite for the attainment
of this study, is method; which not only aids the
memory, but assists the judgement in fixing the
dependence of one event on another.   Geog-
raphy and Chronology (which last is the funda-
mental art of historical arrangement) are indis-
pensable, for, without the chronological division
... confusion and perplexity must attend
that understanding, in which the annals of passed
ages are not successively linked.   Indulging the

instruction to themselves.

ANOTHER principal requisite for the attainment of this study, is method; which not only ... the memory, but assists the judgement in fixing the dependence of one event on another. Geography and Chronology, (which last is the fundamental art of historical arrangement) are indispensable for, without the chronological division of time, confusion and perplexity must attend that understanding, in which the annals of passed ages are not successively linked. Indulging the hope that these reflections will make a permanent

m

rning

curity whi

by allegorie

rmed

are invol

penetrate, and ed. They taught, that the world

almost inexplicable; that it never had a beginning, and

would never have an end; they acknowledged

however, a divine Providence, and affirmed

the motions of the heavens were

the

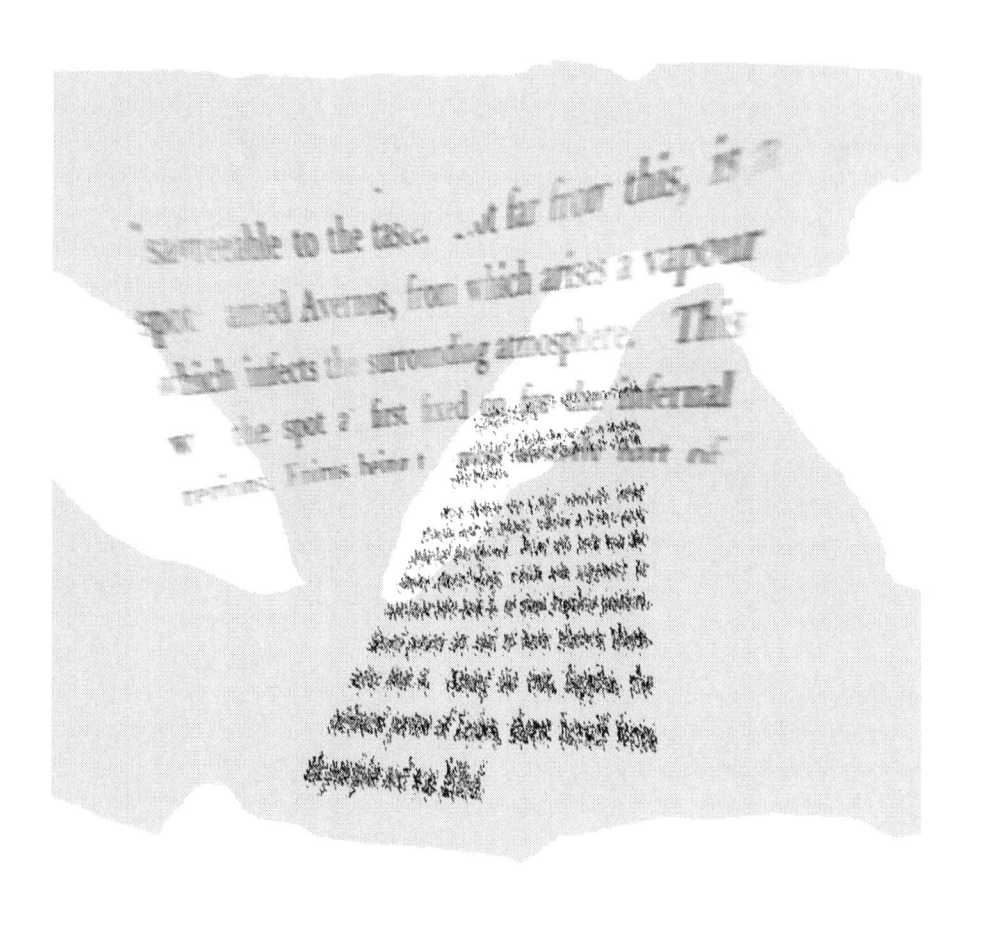

... agreeable to the task ... ot far from this, is a
spot ... amed Avernus, from which arises a vapour
which infects the surrounding atmosphere. This
w... he spot a... first ... infernal
regions. Fuins being ...

Now consider the utterances of Babylonian women.[16]

Mouths marbling

names for mountains.

And what of Telisilla?

Furnishing women with arms, keeping enemies at bay?[17]

16

17

his, tory

SOAKING

VAPOROUS

PRELIMINARY

Let's turn to Nebuchadnezzar.[18]

Bodies thrown
　　onto highways.[19]

Desert secured.[20]

18　Truth, says Wilson (p. 43), condemns ~~VICE~~.

19　Brings to mind ~~(memory)~~~~(method)~~~~(breathing)~~
other ~~HIGHWAYS~~ | ~~(other deserts)~~
　　　　| ~~BODIES~~　~~(our fellow creatures)~~~~(mostlywomen)~~
　　　　　　~~DISCARDED~~ | ~~(others' beloveds)~~
　　| |　　| ~~DISAPPEARED~~ |
　　(sometimesfound)(ornot)(later)(summed|up)
　　　(as acronyms) **MMIWG** | ~~&~~ | ~~etc.~~ **CONJURED** |
(thrumming) (*Reflections on the Errors*
to be met with in History | beneath | it | all)

20

I'm running

(through Chronological Haze)

each breath

| ~~AN~~ | ~~ENDLESS~~ | | | | ~~MIRAGE~~

Now,

reflect on mortal wounds,
tombs with sublime inscriptions,

and grief,[21]

real and fictitious.[22]

---

21 What are we to make of *LETTER XXXV—*?

22

If *REAL*

(then ~~GRIEF~~ | ought not | to be limited to time).
(See p. 287)

If *FICTITIOUS*

(then ~~GRIEF~~ | ought not to be | prolonged).
(See p. 287)

(See Wilson's account of Lacedaemon) (those who grieved for 11 days.)

And don't forget the scarlet cloaks,

worn to disguise flowing blood.[23] [24]

---

23 Let's ask | the | *KNOWLEDGE KEEPERS*:

Oh,   when |

       is *GRIEF*

~~EVER NOT REAL?~~

Oh,   when | | |

   is *A LIFE*,

         (thousands |of | lives) | | | | | ||| |

   unfinished,

     ~~ever finite?~~

24 also, the **RED** ~~DRESSES~~

The word "resilience"

never appears in Wilson's history. [25] [26]

---

25 Although **FAVORABLE WINDS**

and the *FEROCITY* of wolves do.

(p. 120) (p. 252)

(also, the word *'STRONG'*, appearing 18 times)

(mostly to describe | holds | garrisons || invading armies |

| | testimonies|) (pp 40, 54, 61, etc.)

26 (I like to think) (if it were up to Wilson)

we'd be ~~RUNNING~~

ahead of

advancing ~~FORCES,~~

CENTURIES,

~~REPEATED.~~

You ask about wild beasts, inventions,

diversity of tongues,[27]

    and beginnings.[28]

---

[27]

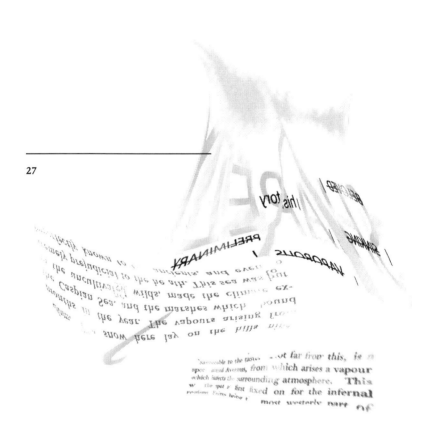

[28] On page 6, Wilson tells us that ~~MEN~~ and ~~EMPIRES~~ FIRST APPEARED IN THE EAST.

This is History.^{29 30 31}

---

29   The dark, euphemistic face of the Euxine Sea.

     Herod, angel-smitten, worm-devoured.

30   A woman wrapped in a **WHITE CLOAK**,

     a *CURIOUSLY-ENGRAVED ROSE* on her ring,

     her long hair falling

31   (nameless) (eventually disappeared)

     her (unforgivable) capacity | for translating

     the *WEIGHT* of Empires

     ~~PRIVATE TRAUMAS~~.

History, a whirlpool,[32]

sucking in obscure circumstances

with a frightful noise.[33]

---

32 **SUBTERRANEAN PASSAGES**

going | where?

33 *TRAVELERS* (says Wilson)

have corrected the error

(told by the Ancients)

about

ENORMOUS

~~SERPENTS~~.

After p. 316.

the end of my |BELOVED| |AVOWED| |SINKING| **HISTORY**,
will I remain

      yours
           (affectionately)?[34]

34

calamitous | mankind's

(~~OUTWARD~~ flow) (banishment) (armies marching

under MOONLIGHT)

VAPOROUS, SHAPELY | | bre|a|k|s|)

goddesses and **SHIPWRECKED** strangers

(sacrificed) (eventually)

(leap off | completion's line |

35

36

37

---

35 History.

36   There can be no abstemious recounting.

Take up your **NAPTHA-TIPPED** arrow.

Let loose your bow-shot | bituminous | ~~MEMORY~~,

37   and, lofty (with aspiring and immense liberty),

endure, ~~LIVING IN SECURITY~~, flourishing,

your reign over *WIND-TOSSED SEAS*

putting illness and calendars

TO FLIGHT.

38

---

38 I ~~REMAIN~~, &c.

hopeful | you will | never | | regret

| the | time |

spent| in ~~BELOVED~~'s | ~~ATTAINMENT~~.

Portrait of a Lady

1996 film adaptation of the Henry James novel starring
Nicole Kidman. Jane Campion, director.

Scent and stray hairs. Rain against wrinkled skin, running in
rivulets through the soft ridges, umbrella forgotten. Solidity of
a foot in a running shoe, crossed over ankle. Bag of groceries
gathered up to one's chest. Small gestures that protect and define.
Women locking eyes on the Metro, our reflections in the glass
as the train pulls into McGill, overlaid against a black-and-white
photograph of a model in white cotton underwear. Merging, the
blur of the train's movement, shifting kaleidoscope, red diamonds,
opal rectangles, adamantine pears, blue eyes. When afternoon
light deepens and shadows thicken, when the air crystallizes, and
her body shifts into slow motion, running through the clearing
and up the snow-covered walkway towards the house, the pleats
of the long skirt rippling, up the snow-covered steps, her hand on
the door latch, the room inside glowing orange from the fireplace,
finding the door locked, and turning, turning around and looking.

The Moses

Michelangelo's sculpture of the biblical Moses,
c. 1513 – 1515; height 92.5 inches, San Pietro in Vincoli

morning flags on balconies blue sky white furious clouds,
         openness and boundary a network of birds

think about ascending the old staircase, lining up to see the Moses,
         immensity of stone dropped inside you
         calling itself belief

someone tells you forget God. new songbird in the trees
         looping melodies at 3:30 AM

think about the feast of geranium petals, red swoon
         across the lawn

    the streaming hair, carved from stone, yet spilling,
         coiling, through the veined, marble hand

    and holograph trees,
wind-fevered on blinds
         your niece asleep on the couch, the soles of her feet

It was like that Hilary Swank movie

1999 Academy-award-winning movie based on the real-life story
of Brandon Teena, a trans man from Lincoln Nebraska whose death
was the result of a violent hate crime.

Sky coal black and town bunkered down for the night. Circle in

closer and you can't miss it. That figure splayed on the cold earth

outside the factory. That's Lana. Telltale sign: endearing brown mole

on her left breast. The boy with his head between her legs, pretty

as a girl, that's Brandon. Circle of Brandon's mouth, sweet as

molasses. Circle of Lana's sigh, ephemeral as a smoke ring.

Never one to put the cart before the horse, Brandon is only now

hitching that dildo from his pants. Come closer, and see it

disappear inside Lana. *It's not real*, someone in the audience

mutters. The power lines hum: *yes it is*. And Lana breaks into

circles of light. I could tell you more. Like how, at the karaoke

bar, Brandon's spirit was silver, and Lana saw it shine because she

had that spirit too. How, in another scene, Brandon's fake penis

is visible, on Lana's bed, as he binds his breasts in front of Lana's

mirror. Or how it ends: Tom, Lana's former boyfriend, arriving with a pistol to teach Brandon that transubstantiation always

has a consequence. Tom and Peter are convicted for the rape

and murder of Brandon Teena and Lana leaves town. As she drives

away, "The Bluest Eyes in Texas" plays on the radio and power

lines criss-cross overhead. I can feel the highway unspooling, and

I don't need dialogue to know she plans to leave it all behind,

to forget the boy whose sex was like hers. Two winged smudges

in perpetual flight at the apex of his legs.

2666

The last novel by Roberto Bolaño, published in 2004 one year after the author's death. The novel circles around the murders of women in Santa Teresa, based on the real femicides in Juárez, Mexico.

He doesn't want to say how many have been found.
How many have not.
The first book of his story is the Via Rail train
crossing the Precambrian shield, windows flashing sunset.
The second book is the skyline, tree-ribbed.
The third, deer at clearing's edge.
The fourth book is the sentimental song,
the one that gives back his teenage years, the malls
where kids disperse their grief and anger.
The fifth book is an old man walking down a back alley,
observed by a German Shepherd so regularly beaten by its owner
it became afraid of any person passing,
even long after they were gone from sight.

Musée des Beaux Arts

The Montréal Museum of Fine Arts, established in 1860, is the largest
museum, by gallery space, in Canada. It also contains Canada's oldest
art library.

I move back and forth
from The Group of Seven: 1921, 'The First Show'
(a nation's pride) to 1928 (even prouder), from painting:
"It is similar to English landscapes," to painting:
blowing snow, road lime green
      brown ruts, wheat hot pink, village shacks chugging waves
sticks branches stepping back into the guard
   men in blue who watch nervously, will we
     touch the paintings? will we try
to touch?

    Harris, Jackson, Carmichael, slanted rectangles,
blue-orange, wine-red, dim aura of a streetlight, over and over,
   today I wanted only images, no words—
the sky's dark light, vine-colored
    wall, each magnification revealing new
detail, patterns discovered at larger scales,
a geometry of precision. "I am a collage

of unaccounted for brushstrokes. I am
     all random." (Stockard Channing, at the chi-chi dinner party,
Six Degrees of Separation. She walks out, leaves the party.
   Leaves him. An art-dealer, played by Donald Sutherland).
  Diminishing perspective,
     the brushstrokes (up close) are
      phrases, violet splintered through with chartreuse,
    undercut by transitional hues,

(the film ends with her walking away, down a
New York street),
the active voice of red
astonishes, the body's undulations, hinge
(movement),

gliding, apposition of flat, or slightly
curved surfaces, adjoining bones move back and forth in
calligraphic strokes, entrance hallway, heels clicking lightly
against the floor. The stairs in the Musée des Beaux Arts
are structured in such a manner as to slow down
the climber's upward movement, inducing
a momentary pause
(freeze-frame)
in the middle of each step taken,
ascension of schoolboys (class visit)
green crewnecks/navy trousers,
their bodies attempt to navigate
(articulate)
the staircase,

heads bob conscious
of slow-motion extension,
destinations (Cafeteria, Gift Shop)   elongated,
no longer sharp pinpoints of light ahead in the distance,
(elevation, hope, flexion), knees angular,
toes
en pointe,
synovial pirouette
(laughter),
they master the staircase.

Like that planet in my film

Melancholia, a 2011 science fiction film by Danish film director
Lars von Trier.

The bus careens towards an apocalypse.
The road ends, you get out.
Inside the house, through the living room window, the ocean,
getting bigger, approaching.
Like that planet in my film, a voice says.
Danish accent.
Lars? Is that you?
JA. Det er mig.
But—you don't fly. How did you get here?
It's a dream, min ven.
Waves break against the shore.
Together you sit cross-legged on the sand and begin to clap.

FATA MORGANA

"… short as a sigh … life is a dream."
OMAR KHAYYÁM

I exist in a time

when small gestures from dreams

materialize in the day

like tufts of wool caught on a fence

while nearby graze the sheep.

You wake from a dream
you didn't know had claimed you.
Car heading down the highway.
What day is it? you ask.
Thursday, the driver says.
You reach out, his shoulder your anchor.
No, the date.
Turns out you've lost months.
Your fear an algal bloom, each breath a protest.

*

The structure is frail, unsealed,
extreme height visible through cracks.
The way to leave no longer easy.
She finishes the painting.
Illusion (firm footing) returns.
The miraculous move down the stairwell.

*

You walk the empty streets of a town
awash in the vitreous fluids
of an eye that weeps.

Take the stairs
to the second floor of the house.
She's in the bedroom at the end of the hallway.

Her stick arms reach for you,
her long teeth click like a metronome.
You know better
than to cross the threshold.

Waves in the old glass window
bend afternoon light
and the horizon, a wild beast,
lengthens its stride.

*

She came to you last night.
Alba deer, she said.
Sweet whiteclover.
Desert survivor.

You took her hands,
looked into her eyes.
Just as it always was.

Alba deer, she said.
Our own whiteclover day.
Two years.
Desert survivor.

*

Other side of night porous
with its shadows of leaves
and gauze phantasm window.
You want to cry out, but you can't.
You're between bells and wars,
mute in the magma.

*

Enter the chamber, following the sound of her voice.
Each chamber is separated by doors,
and each door, once you step through, seals itself behind you.
You find her in the deepest chamber.
She climbs onto your back.
You retrace your steps, through all the doors, chambers.
Find the way out.
Let's have lunch, she says.
I'm hungry.

*

I sit on the edge of the bed.

I see you, I say.

I know you do, hon, she says.

She holds out her hand.

I take it in mine.

Your dream, I say. Tell me.

I dreamt there was world peace, she says.

So I tell you to open the back door

and you do. We can hear everyone celebrating.

We find summer.

We find the yellow car.

The trailer. Everything.

The moving trees, the wind.

She squeezes my hand.

It's really my dream, isn't it? I say.

She smiles, nods.

It's okay, hon, she says.

*

Loop

After sense of motion in the horizon. The mind going somewhere. Blue wave, proximity of stars, words, tenderness. The way the robin calls the early hour, ephemeral and absolute. After intuition flows from dark to earth. After asking what's real. The plenary rustle of leaves at the corner of 5th Avenue. Accidental joy and the way light flows onto a building before the sky's separated itself from the land and the church spire. After we look sideways, not straight-on. After history takes us by halves. Provocation, tribes, and birch trees in sunlight. The resurrected moon rolling back the gated year. A word's familiar bend when you were comforted. An across-the-room hello pulsating the spine. Reprieve, emptiness, and flickering thought. Lines and enjambments, crossings and dots, worked by hands to replace tree-green prairies with words. Stars, vapour, salt, dust, seed, smoke. A beginning, the beginning, or beginnings. After lovers shape the dawn, willful through decades of evolution. Even after what light has seen of you. By this I mean the fragile geography of connection. Each embodied now. Each aphonic purple low-lit cloud, skirting the horizon. That lake trout, gleam of eye, staring up from the bottom of the milk carton. The cicada, seventeen years underground, living for only three weeks above. The moment when longing is no longer longing but something else. Sunlight ephemera on living room walls. The river's leafed estuary. The gutted sky where a raven floats weightless.

THE SPEED OF THIS PASSING

… I would say that nothing is too slow, or too brief,
for the universe, I would say that naming is still
a function of dreaming and of hope.

NICOLE BROSSARD

2019

The sparrows refuse to retrain themselves.
                              Flying away
in mighty astonishment every time I appear at the window.

Regrouping in the winter vine
ceaseless, their movements, as sunlight shifts
cadenced heat.

Eyes insist, space replies
in sparrowed metaphor.

Hands cupped round
a word.

Naming

1.

    She stood there for three days in the corner
of the room. Giving me every piece of wisdom. Then she smiled
and moved on. A shadow between me
    and the not-quite-there moon. Her housecoat billowing
in folds around her.

    That Montréal summer,
stained sumptuous with berries and pleasure, her face tilted up
    toward the trees, their frieze of colour, crazy reds
rushing amongst the greens. Howling over those awful sayings
of my uncle's. "She's built like a Dutch plow—kind of thick
where the pin goes in" and "Thanks (pronounced tanks)
don't fill my gas tank."

We slowed down into a rhythm, almost matched. That afternoon,
when we opened the windows, ladybugs—
  their red shells
    against the glass—

If there were a volcanic eruption
and we were trapped in molten lava, a series of hieroglyphic marks
    and wave patterns would have been found around us,
the rooms of our story made clear.

2.

Raven floats oceanic in the sky, glistening wave
of black wings, now strangely mammoth, stationary
on the low branch outside the window
    before swooping down to pluck up the dead baby bird
I'd asked the neighbor to come and remove.

    Each day passes. Patiently,
night erases itself. I'm not worried
about what happens to me after, my mother says.
I'm worried about leaving people behind.
    Sporadic bee on the other side of the screen wants in.
    I ask the bee for time, still more time.

3.

I come inside from raking and fertilizing the lawn.
                  I'll never garden again, she says.
My heart is broken, she says.
This is a woman who does not
make pronouncements.
             In the doorway,
I command the tears in my eyes to retract, like rabbits when
they reabsorb their litter.

4.

Her body, part-here, part-elsewhere.
Beneath my hands, as I massage,
     skin liquid softness riddled with tumorous lumps,
this anatomy of touch is a listening mirror we hold up to the day.
     If my mother's body were a song, the refrain would be:
Transform! Transform! Transform!
     In the bathroom, she looks up to find her face.

5.

Before bed, she sits in the chair looking out onto the garden.

We have nesting wrens—a first.
    And the bark-coloured buddha placed
beneath the elm, another first.

I want to go, she says.
I'm ready.

6.

Each time we die god cleans our brains,
        my 8-year-old niece announces.

I love how children know dying
is like air wind light.

Always there, this event, always
approaching, existing, longing, impending, becoming.
        And yet, it's June, and our eyes seek out
            the Siberian irises in the back yard,
                they've grown
at least one foot
        in only two days.

7.

Remember my hand.
Here, touching the corner of the dresser.

    I will.

Keep the lace curtain on the bedroom window.

    Always.

In the backyard,
from her wheelchair, watching me do yard work,
she reaches out, hands suspended in the air.

I don't know
    what she wants, lean in,
      she takes my face in her hands. Thank you, she whispers.
Her face translucent,
        its expression something beyond
          sadness, some wordless thing
beyond herself, the change
    she is becoming.

If the measure of love is loss, why not live in it, this light?

Spindle of light turns in the corner of the room.

Window frames blue
where clouds read the sky awake.

      This I know:
the dead are not gone. They are present.
Their ephemeral absoluteness made from
refraction, bone, sight.
Curve of her head, sea-shadows.

What I mean to say is

she read the bible as poetry, because poetry
requires surrender, acceptance
 that for every feeling a thought must form and then pass,
yes, she embraced the separateness that folds
everything together, gave herself over to each caress,
 hug, kiss, visit, knowing intimacy
would eventually become
  sky.
 I watched as she let a new language invent its passage,
while also reviving an old language,
  openness and boundary,
her consciousness expanding to envelop plan A, plan B,
 direction south, body and land,
loved ones,
   scattering of clouds.

Quietus

Heaven, you say, this is heaven.
We sit in lawn chairs in the back yard,
and what I have always called a horse wind—
   rare, this childhood wind, bringing
    its unspecified scent of freedom—
moves through the garden and the summer evening.

Motherfield

Breaking blue, let it in.
Louvered edge of the rise is for me,
        peripheral bloom of passage.
So close, I could ask its name.

Night's uncoveredness
        beyond the building; it knows
        how to lift the line.

Slight waver of tree branches.
I turn and follow the concrete ledge
        along the grooved wall that holds the stairwell
        out back.

Curious corners trace pale dome.
        Sky loosening, white clouded.

Call it cicatrice, and it's rhythm.

Keep silent, it's a star.

Thumbprint moon erases itself from east,
        flock of balconies, pale undersides
against the not-yet-there sky.

I can't see it, only apprehend its gesture—
      derelict wingspan,
      descent through shadow.

Rise, I think, like pine trees in a boreal forest.
Back to the river, I think, like the lab frogs in *ET*.

I'm in the day as I wait.
Elm tree has no regret.
Small light inside reflects.

I can't hear it, only sense its reach,
    telluric and tender.

NOTES

"Loop" poems
These are inspired by Nicole Brossard's "Soft Link" poems in
Notebook of Roses and Civilization, Coach House Books, 2007.

*

ARTERIAL
The Brossard epigraph is from "Process of a Yes its energy in
progress" in *Fluid Arguments: Essays*. The Mercury Press, 2005. Used
with permission of the author.

*

"The Return"
For the opening section, see the "I" section of Anne Caron's "The
Glass Essay" in *Glass, Irony and God*. The "Body" section utilizes
information found in Fishes: *Their Journeys and Migrations* by Louis
Roule, specifically pages 7, 93, 95.

*

"Clouds"
The quote, "I am here," is Czeslaw Miolsz, *To begin where I am:
Selected Essays*.

*

"Birthmarked"
"Dawn is buffalo in the fog" and "the moon is the closest I can
get to it." See Jack Gilbert's poem "Finding Something" in *The
Great Fires*. The D. H. Lawrence reference is from his essay, "New
Mexico."

*

"On the Road near the Crest of a Hill"
See Robert Hass, "On the Coast near Sausalito," in *The Apple Trees
at Olema*. The poet quoted—"to release the sound"—is, I believe,
Erín Moure, from *My Beloved Wager: Essays from a Writing Practice*.

*

QUARRY
The Erín Moure epigraph is from "The Anti-Anæsthetic" in *My
Beloved Wager: Essays from a Writing Practice*. NeWest Press, 2009.
Used with permission of the author.

*

my | B̶E̶L̶O̶V̶E̶D̶ | **HISTORY** |
This section is in direct conversation with *Letters on Ancient History*
by Anne Wilson, with language, and occasional phrases, pulled
directly from the 1809 textbook.

The mountain-like shape which floats throughout this section,
often providing a structural container for vaporous textual
appearances, is an outline of the iceberg that sunk the Titanic.

*

FATA MORGANA

The Omar Khayyám epigraph is from *Rubaiyat Of Omar Khayyam: English, French And German Translations Comparatively Arranged V2*.

*

THE SPEED OF THIS PASSING

The Brossard epigraph is from "Process of a Yes its energy in progress" in *Fluid Arguments: Essays*. The Mercury Press, 2005. Used with permission of the author.

ACKNOWLEDGMENTS

Thank you to the Saskatchewan Arts Board and the Canada Council for the Arts for funding that helped me to write this manuscript.

*

Some of the poems have been published in *CV2*, *Tessera* and *Grain*, as well as garnering a place in the CBC Poetry Prize Longlist 2020.

*

Many thanks to Liz Philips, for believing in me and in my writing.

*

Special thanks to Anne Simpson, who helped me to open up, with surprise and wonder, to what this book needed and wanted to be, who nudged, pointed, encouraged and repeated, in the most lovely and profound - the most magical - of ways. I'm forever grateful, dear Anne.

*

Deep gratitude to Maria Campbell for helping me to learn about my first father, Don Nielson, and my Métis history, for building the road and walking on it, and for making me laugh.

Many thanks to Sylvia Legris and Jeanette Lynes, who have generously given me various forms of writerly encouragement along the long way. Also, a dear thank you to Randy Lundy for his close reading of and comments on "Birthmarked" and "Clouds."

*

Much gratitude to Kathie Pruden, for listening and understanding.

*

Warm thanks to friends, Trevor Greenbank, Jo Wastell, Francesca LoDico, Neil Greening, and Gloria Stefanson, for being there.

*

For love, support, and inspiration—for your bravery, curiosity, creativity, beauty, and kindness—for your ongoing presence—my sweet mother, I thank you. This is for you.

Diana Hope Tegenkamp is a Métis writer who lives and creates on Treaty 6 Territory, Homeland of the Métis. Her writing has appeared in numerous literary journals across Canada, including *CV2*, *Grain*, and *Matrix*, to name a few. In 2020, she was awarded second prize in the Banff Centre Bliss Carmen Poetry Contest and was longlisted for the CBC Poetry Prize.

Diana works across mediums, including film, photography, visual art, performance art, sound and music. Her video performance piece, UN-MUTE, was selected for SLANT's 2021 Writing Bodies festival, and more of her multi-disciplinary work, including film poems for *Girl running*, can be found on her website, www.dianahopetegenkamp.com.